MW01404907

This Notebook belongs to:

NAME:______________________________

Copyright © 2019 All rights reserved.

Made in the USA
Middletown, DE
28 January 2022

59934695R00066